FIESTA!

FIESTA!

CINCO DE MAYO

Festivals and Holidays

By June Behrens

Photographs by Scott Taylor

A Golden Gate Junior Book   Childrens Press • Chicago

To Edward Stanley

ACKNOWLEDGEMENT

The author wishes to acknowledge with thanks the assistance of Mario Valdez, Olvera Street, Los Angeles, in the development of this manuscript

Library of Congress Cataloging in Publication Data

Behrens, June.
  Fiesta!

  (Festivals and holidays)
  "A Golden Gate junior book."
  SUMMARY: Describes the commemoration of the victory of the Mexican army over the French army on May 5, 1862, a victory which signaled the end of foreign invasions of North America.
    1. Cinco de Mayo (Mexican holiday)—Juvenile literature.
2. Cinco de Mayo, Battle of, 1862—Juvenile literature.
[1. Cinco de Mayo (Mexican holiday) 2. Holidays] I. Taylor, Scott. II. Title.
F1233.B39   1978   394.2'684'72   78-8468
ISBN 0-516-08815-7

FIESTA!

We hear music, music everywhere.
We sing and dance and eat and
    play.
The fiesta in our park is like a
    big party.
Welcome to the fiesta!

Many people wear bright and
    beautiful Mexican costumes.
Look at the sombreros Joe and his
    friends are wearing.
A sombrero is a hat with a very
    broad brim.
It is almost as big as little Joe.

This is a Cinco de Mayo fiesta
    party.
Cinco de Mayo means fifth
    of May.
The fifth of May is a joyous
    festival day, a very special day
    for Mexican Americans.
It is an important day for all the
    people in America.

On May 5, 1862, there was a big
　　battle in the town of Puebla,
　　Mexico.
In a battle with the French army
　　the poor, ragged Mexican
　　army won a great victory.

The victory helped to drive
    foreigners out of North
    America.
No foreign power has invaded
    North America since.
Each year, on the fifth of May,
    people celebrate the victory
    of Cinco de Mayo.

On the great outdoor stage in our
    park dancers in ruffled skirts
    clap their hands.
The music is fast and exciting.
The dancers stamp their feet and
    whirl around.
We sit on the hillside and watch
    the show.

Musicians walk around our park.
They play their guitars and violins
    and trumpets.
They are called Mariachi
    musicians.
When they sing, they give a happy
    little yell.
Yi...Yi...yiyyyyyyyyy!

There are good smells everywhere.
Mothers and fathers make tortillas
in the food stand.
Tortillas look like thin, flat
pancakes.
Father folds the tortilla in the
middle and fills it with beans
and lettuce and tomatoes.
Sometimes he adds hot sauce, too.

On stage, little señoritas and
　　　their partners dance for us.
The mariachis play.
Everyone claps and sings the
　　　lively song.

At school everyone joins in the
    Cinco de Mayo holiday fiesta.
We decorate our school with the
    colors of the Mexican flag—
    green, red and white.
We hang the flag outside.

We have Cinco de Mayo contests
and games.
The most fun of all is the taco-
eating contest!

We decorate our fiesta booths
with Mexican tissue paper
flowers.
We take turns playing with
Mexican toys and games.
We even dig for Mexican
archeological treasures.

We make flour tortillas.
We mix flour, salt and baking
    powder together.
Then we add oil and water.
We make little dough balls and
    roll them out flat.
Then we cook them in a pan.
Delicious!

Fathers and mothers come to see
    our Cinco de Mayo programs.
We sing Mexican songs and do
    special dances.
Our mothers and fathers like the
    beautiful Mexican murals we
    have painted.

All day and into the evening we
      celebrate Cinco de Mayo.
We have a piñata party in the
      evening.
The piñata is a clay pot
      decorated with bright-colored
      tissue paper.
Piñatas are made in many shapes
      and sizes.
Our piñata is a giant star.
It is filled with candy!

The piñata hangs from a rope
    above the heads of boys
    and girls.
Joe is blindfolded and given a
    stick.
He swings again and again at the
    hanging piñata.
At last he hits it.
Candies fly everywhere and
    scatter on the ground.
Everyone scrambles for a piece.

Cinco de Mayo is over until
    next year.
Our Mexican American friends
    have taught us songs and
    games.
They have taught us dances and
    Spanish words.
Amigo means friend.
Everyone has been a good amigo
    on Cinco de Mayo.

Viva la fiesta!

Each year on the fifth of May Mexican-Americans throughout the length and breadth of of our land celebrate their greatest national holiday, *Cinco de Mayo*. For it was on May 5, 1862, in the town of Puebla, Mexico, that the ragged little Mexican army defeated the superior French forces and drove a foreign power from this continent. The holiday is meaningful for all Americans because, since then, no foreign nation has dared to invade these shores. Written for primary grade readers and profusely illustrated with color photographs, *Fiesta!* captures the spirit of all *Cinco de Mayo* celebrations. We see the festivities taking place in a park where young and old alike listen to the music of a Mariachi band and watch the colorfully clad dancers perform traditional Mexican dances. We look in on a school where all the children take part in *Cinco de Mayo* activities—from the taco-eating contest to the breaking of the piñata. *Fiesta!* provides a rich reading experience by bringing to life a holiday which should be known and respected by children everywhere.

JUNE BEHRENS has a rich background of experience from which to draw in meeting the reading needs of primary age children. For many years a reading specialist in one of California's largest public school systems, she has also worked in a large number of bi-lingual school programs and has done extensive graduate work in Mexican-American history. A native Californian, Mrs. Behrens graduated from the University of California at Santa Barbara and obtained her Master's degree from the University of Southern California. She also holds a Credential in Early Childhood Education. She is the author of many books for young children, ranging in subject matter from Colonial history to contemporary biography. She lives with her husband in Redondo Beach near Los Angeles.